NATIVE AMERICAN DOCTOR

NATIVE AMERICAN DOCTOR

The Story of Susan LaFlesche Picotte

Jeri Ferris

Carolrhoda Books, Inc., Minneapolis

For my uncle Fred M. Chase
With memories of Nebraska

Text copyright © 1991 by Jeri Ferris

This book is available in two editions:
Library binding by Carolrhoda Books, Inc.,
   a division of Lerner Publishing Group
Soft cover by First Avenue Editions,
   an imprint of Lerner Publishing Group
241 First Avenue North
Minneapolis, MN 55401 U.S.A.

Website address: www.lernerbooks.com

Library of Congress Cataloging-in-Publication Data

Ferris, Jeri.
   Native American doctor : the story of Susan LaFlesche Picotte /
Jeri Ferris.
      p.   cm.
   Includes bibliographical references and index.
   Summary: A biography of the young Omaha Indian woman who became the first Native American woman to graduate from medical school.
   ISBN 0-87614-443-1 (lib. bdg. : alk. paper)
   ISBN 0-87614-548-9 (pbk. : alk. paper)
   1. Picotte, Susan LaFlesche, 1865–1915—Juvenile literature.
2. Physicians—Nebraska—Biography—Juvenile literature. 3. Omaha Indians—Biography—Juvenile literature. 4. Women physicians—Nebraska—Biography—Juvenile literature. [1. Picotte, Susan LaFlesche, 1865–1915. 2. Women physicians. 3. Physicians. 4. Omaha Indians—Biography. 5. Indians of North America—Biography.] I. Title.
R154.P53F47   1991
610'.92—dc20
[B]   90-28503
[92]

Manufactured in the United States of America
9 10 11 12 13 14 – JR – 07 06 05 04 03 02

Contents

"By day and by night she dreamed dreams and saw visions of larger and better things yet to be done for her beloved people," said the Reverend D.E. Jenkins, Presbyterian Board of Home Missions, about Susan LaFlesche Picotte.

Foreword

At a time when modern medicine was suspect and usually absent on the rolling Nebraska prairie lands of the Omahas, there appeared a frail and hauntingly beautiful Indian woman who opened her medical practice to all, Indian and non-Indian alike, and treated their ailments for a generation. Hardly an Omaha was living who had not been treated by her, and hundreds of white people as well owed their lives to her care. Her intellectual accomplishments, her generosity, and her humanitarian achievements beg for an explanation. The explanation is in this book.

At Susan's funeral service in 1915, the closing prayer was given in the Omaha language by an elder of the tribe, and among the many tributes to her was this by Harry Keefe, an attorney. "We are confronted here with a character rising to greatness and to great deeds, out of conditions which seldom produce more than mediocre men and women, achieving great and beneficent ends over obstacles almost insurmountable."

Susan truly had faced obstacles above and beyond those faced by nineteenth-century white women, yet she overcame every one and dedicated her life to her grateful people. Her story is a litany of frontier vignettes of which classic legends are made, and it needs no embellishment. Dr. Susan could very well emerge as one of the more notable heroines in American history.

My great-grandfather Richard Hastings attended Hampton Institute with her.

Dennis Hastings
Omaha Tribe Historian

Introduction

In 1865, when Susan LaFlesche of the Omaha Indians was born, the Plains Indian life of tipis and buffalo hunts was almost over. The buffalo herds were disappearing.

Only a few years before, there had been a reason to learn the ceremonies and prayers that brought the buffalo and the elk, the corn and the squash. Only a few years before, Wakon'da, the Great Spirit who created all living things, had provided buffalo by the ten millions—so many buffalo that the prairie was black with their shaggy bodies.

Every child had had a part in helping the family live. The boys learned to make and use the weapons that would provide buffalo meat and protect their village. The girls learned to make buffalo skins into tipis and moccasins and clothing, and to prepare enough food to last the long, hard winter. Every child was a part of the whole circle of land, sky, winds, sun, and moon.

And then their world changed.

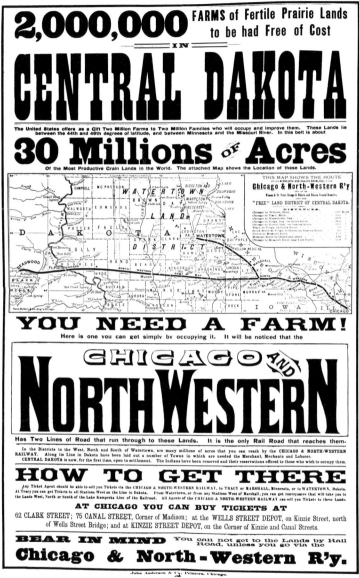

By the late 1800s, the buffalo were vanishing, and the "empty" and fertile plains were the promised land for farmers who came from as far away as Germany. In fact the Homestead Act of 1862, which gave 160 acres of free land to anyone (anyone but an Indian) who said he or she would farm it *guaranteed* that there would be a flood of white settlers spreading far over the prairie.

White traders brought guns, calico, alcohol, and disease. White hunters killed buffalo for their woolly coats and their tasty tongues, and just for the fun of it. White settlers built houses and farms on the Indians' unending prairie. Few of these new people seemed to care that the land was already taken. Anyway, they said, the "savages" don't know how to use this land as it was meant to be used.

Representatives of the president in Washington, D.C., came with a message for the Indians who lived on the Plains, the land between the Rocky Mountains and the Mississippi River. They told the Indians that the president was their "Great White Father." Soldiers sent by the Indians' new "father" pushed the Plains Indians onto smaller and smaller pieces of land. And the Great White Father promised his "children" some land they could own "as long as the grass shall grow and the waters shall run."

The Indians didn't understand these promises. They believed the land couldn't be owned by a person any more than the rain could be owned. They didn't like to be called children, either. "We are grown men, like you," they said to the men from Washington.

But the fate of the Plains Indians was no longer up to the Indians, it was in the hands of Indian agents, all of them white. These agents did what the government back in Washington told them to do. And the government said the Indians would have to go.

In 1854 leaders from nine Plains tribes went by train to Washington, D.C. They signed treaties giving up

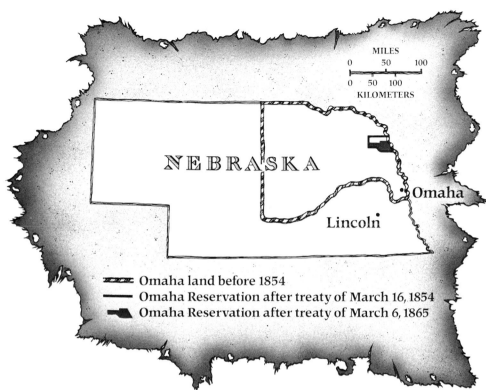

MILES
0   50   100

0   50   100
KILOMETERS

NEBRASKA

• Omaha

Lincoln

Omaha land before 1854
Omaha Reservation after treaty of March 16, 1854
Omaha Reservation after treaty of March 6, 1865

Omaha lands once covered about one-third of what would become the state of Nebraska. In 1854 the Omahas gave up almost 6,000,000 acres of land, at less than one-half cent per acre, in return for a reservation of 300,000 acres. In 1865 the Omahas sold part of the northern half of their reservation to the Winnebago Indians.

most of their rich, fertile hunting land in exchange for reservations—sections of land set aside for them.

The reservation system was supposed to solve, for white people, the conflict caused by whites settling on Indian land. There were some whites who believed the solution was simply to destroy all Indians. But most white people did understand that the Indians had been there first and should have some land of their own to live on—not, of course, the *best* land. The Omahas were assigned a 300,000-acre section of land in northeastern Nebraska, bordering the Missouri River.

Once they had been moved to reservations, the Plains Indian men were told that they could no longer hunt to provide meat and skins for their families or fight to defend their tribes. They were to become farmers instead. Although the Omaha men had always helped the women with corn planting and harvesting when it was necessary, they were not farmers and they did not want to become farmers. But they were not given a choice.

It was as if the floor had fallen from under their feet. All the values and beliefs that had fit together and worked before, now didn't. The Plains Indians' traditional way of life was destroyed.

I
A Young Omaha Girl

On June 17, 1865, a little girl was born in Nebraska on the Omaha Reservation. The tiny baby with the big brown eyes was the child of Iron Eye, chief of the Omahas, and his wife, The One Woman. They named their new baby Susan. Susan was welcomed by three sisters: Susette, whose Omaha name was Bright Eyes, age eleven; Rosalie, age four; and Marguerite, age three.

Although Susan's father was the Omaha chief, he was only part Omaha. Iron Eye, whose English name was Joseph LaFlesche, was the son of a French father and an Omaha or Ponca mother. He was fluent in French and several Indian languages, and when he was young, he had traveled extensively with his father, who was a trader. In 1848, when Iron Eye was a grown man of about twenty-eight, he was adopted by Chief Big Elk of the Omahas. Big Elk, whose own son was sickly and soon died, announced that he wished Iron Eye to

Joseph (Iron Eye) and Mary Gale (The One Woman) LaFlesche. There is still disagreement among the Omahas as to whether Iron Eye was actually an Omaha. Some believe he was half Ponca rather than half Omaha. However, in the past, the Omahas and the Poncas were considered one tribe; and though later tribal politics separated the two, they remain related tribes.

succeed him. Big Elk probably adopted Iron Eye because he saw that Iron Eye had the experience and knowledge necessary to help the Omahas survive in the white world.

The Omaha leaders who preferred to maintain the traditional ways were unhappy with Big Elk's choice. But even so, Iron Eye became chief soon after Big Elk's death in 1853.

Susan's mother, whose English name was Mary Gale, was the daughter of Nicomi, an Omaha-Oto-Iowa Indian woman, and Dr. John Gale of the U.S. Army.

She had gone to school in St. Louis, Missouri, where she had learned to speak French and had also learned about white customs.

Susan, Rosalie, and Marguerite were not given Omaha names, and neither Susan nor her three older sisters received the woman's tattoos (a sun spot on the forehead and a four-pointed star, symbolizing the four life-giving winds, on the throat) that indicated a high rank. These tattoos were an honor among the Omahas, but Chief Iron Eye had decided he did not want his children so marked in a white world.

Iron Eye believed the Omahas would have to learn white ways if they were going to live in the new white world. He himself was one of the Indian leaders who had signed the treaties in Washington in 1854. There he had seen broad cobblestone streets, tall brick buildings, horse-drawn trolley cars, and white people everywhere. "Look ahead," Iron Eye had said when he returned, "and you will see nothing but the white man." He saw that the Omaha way, his way, was forever changed. Of what use now were hunting skills? Of what use now were skills in tanning buffalo skins and drying buffalo meat? Of what use now were dances and prayers to Wakon'da?

So, on a low hill overlooking the rich, flat bottom-land beside the Missouri River, Iron Eye built a two-story wood frame house as a model for a new way of life. He plowed the heavy black soil with a yoke of oxen and divided the land into separate farms. He asked other Omahas to build wooden houses on these farms. This was an enormous step, for at that time the Omaha Indians still lived in traditional earth lodges or in tipis.

The lodges and tipis had worked well for the Omahas' former traditional way of life. An earth lodge was the family's unmovable home. The tipi was the family's portable home, used when traveling over the prairie after the buffalo. It was easy to put up and easy to take down and pack. In fact when it was taken apart, the tipi itself became a sledlike carrier (a travois) that was pulled by a horse. The poles were fastened to the horse's sides, and the tipi cover was folded into a platform on which the family's possessions, as well as babies and old people, were placed.

The traditional ways, however, were changing, and some of the Omahas agreed to try Iron Eye's new way. In a few years, there were nineteen wood frame houses. But not all of the Omahas agreed that white ways meant progress. Those who did not like Iron Eye's ideas, and who still lived in earth lodges or in tipis, called the wooden houses Iron Eye's "make-believe white man's village." Many of them wanted only to be left alone to hunt the buffalo and follow traditional Omaha ways as they always had, as best they could.

Although Iron Eye was willing to learn white ways, he refused to bow to white authority. Susan was only a year old when the new white Indian agent removed her father as chief because Iron Eye wouldn't do what he was told. Iron Eye was replaced with a "reservation

An Omaha village in the mid-1800s, with tipis to the left and an earth lodge to the right

chief," or "paper chief," who would do what the agent wanted. But Iron Eye continued to advise the tribe and was a leader, a chief without the title, until his death years later.

Susie was the youngest in her family. She had warm brown eyes, a sunny smile, heavy long black hair, and big ideas. She followed her sisters as they helped their mother. She swept the wooden floor clean, down to the cracks, with a stick broom that was as tall as she was. She learned how to plant corn and beans and melons, and how to harvest them when the honking geese swept southward across the sky. She learned how to mix pemmican, a food made of meat and fat, and she stood on tiptoe to taste the sweet golden pies her mother made out of squash.

Susie also loved to be with her father. Sometimes she walked quietly behind him as he inspected his fields. Sometimes she ran and skipped in front of him as he cared for his large herd of horses and cattle. And sometimes she stood beside him and listened to the wise advice he gave the tribe, for the duty of a leader was to provide wisdom and to suggest appropriate behavior.

One day Susie heard her father speaking to a shamefaced young man. "He who is present at a wrongdoing and lifts not a hand to prevent it is as guilty as the wrongdoers," Iron Eye said. "When you see a boy barefooted and lame, take off your moccasins and give them to him. When you see a boy hungry, bring him to your house and give him food." This advice stuck firmly in Susie's mind.

Like her father, Susie liked to take charge of things and take care of people. Sometimes her big sisters just had to smile at all the advice Susie gave them, but Susie's friends trotted after her and listened eagerly to her ideas—and her advice.

Susie and her friends loved to play dolls. They would choose a quiet place, safely away from the boys playing in their cornhusk warbonnets or tearing through the village in a game of tag or galloping after imaginary buffalo on imaginary horses. The girls made their dolls out of corncobs or pieces of wood and dressed them in calico left over from their own long skirts. They made tiny cradleboards for the baby dolls, and they built tipis for their doll families with sunflower stalks for the poles and old blankets for the covers. They made play dishes out of clay and mud and little play sleeping mats from the bark of cottonwood trees. Susie would arrange the mats around a make-believe fire in the middle of her play tipi, fold the door flap back, and make her dolls' visitors welcome.

Sometimes the girls played that they were going on an old-time buffalo hunt. They tied the tipi poles to their dogs' sides, folded the tipi cover on top, and made a travois for the dolls. Then off they went, with the excited dogs right behind (usually), each dog dragging its travois with leaps and bounds and a wagging tail.

Susie also loved to hear her half-brother, Francis, who was eight years older than she, describe a *real* buffalo hunt. He knew about them because he had hunted buffalo himself. Susie shivered with excitement as she listened to his stories. She could almost hear the huge buffalo bellowing and thundering across the plains as the earth shook under their pounding hooves and a cloud of dust rose to cover the sun. She could almost feel the rage of the buffalo as they glared with rolling red eyes at the hunters galloping in close enough to kill. She could almost see the dead buffalo, whose skin and meat and horns and hooves would provide food, shelter, and clothing for the Omahas for another year.

Most of all, Susie loved to ride. She rode her pony bareback over the rounded hills and beside the streams lined with willows. She rode past the blacksmith shop and waved at the sweaty smith bent over his fire, and past the corn-grinding mill with its huge stone wheels.

She rode along the wide Missouri River and watched through the cottonwood trees as steamships puffed up the river to stop at the reservation trading post.

Usually Susie and her friends were happy, but sometimes they were miserably hungry and unhappy. The problem was that even though the government had promised to send cattle regularly to make up for the buffalo the Indians weren't supposed to hunt, the food often did not arrive. And even though Iron Eye encouraged his people to become farmers, many of the Omahas were determined to continue in the old ways and follow the buffalo. They did not want to become farmers, and they did not plant crops. So Iron Eye would kill the cattle from his own herds and give the meat to his people. Susie's family harvested vegetables from their garden beside the stream or from their potato or corn patch, and they searched for bushes covered with wild berries. They shared everything they had with those who needed food. Iron Eye often went without food himself so others could have enough. Not only was this the right thing to do, but it was expected of one who was a leader.

II
Prairie Childhood

Nearly ten years before Susie was born, a Presbyterian mission school had been built on the reservation, on a high bluff overlooking the Missouri River. Iron Eye insisted that every one of his children go to the school so that they would become fluent in English and well educated. The first year, 1857, the school had only twenty-five boys and four girls, for although some families had followed Iron Eye's example, not all Omaha families saw a need for the white man's education.

The students were not allowed to speak in Omaha at the school, but only in English. The boys were not allowed to wear their Omaha clothing, but only white man's clothes. One of the goals of the school was to make the Indians as much like whites as possible, and the teachers really believed they were doing it in the best and fastest way. But their methods were painful and

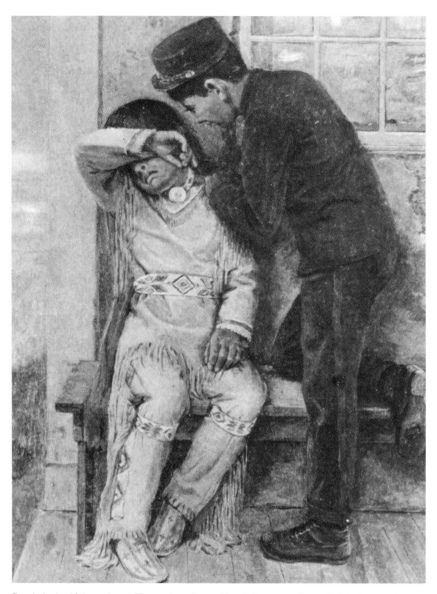

Susie's half-brother, Francis, described how sad and frightened one boy felt on his first day at school. His mother had dressed him in his best clothes: embroidered moccasins and leggings and a little buffalo robe decorated with colorful porcupine quills. But when the boy got to school, he was given heavy shoes and a stiff dark suit with shiny brass buttons. His Indian clothes were sent home in a bundle.

shocking for the children, and they made some families *sure* their children did not need a white education.

Susie started at the mission school when she was very small, so small that if she fell asleep at school, the big boys would gently put her *inside* a desk to finish her nap. The mission school was closed in 1869, when Susie was four. Susette, Susie's oldest sister, left home for more schooling in the East that same year. That fall Susie and her other sisters walked to the new Omaha Agency school, three miles away in the town of Macy, swinging their tin lunch pails and hurrying to get there by nine o'clock. The Omaha Agency was the place where the government agent to the Omahas had his headquarters.

Susie liked school from the first day. She studied geography, history, grammar, spelling, arithmetic, and music, and soon she could read and write in English. When her work was done, she quietly helped the students who got stuck on their problems. When the teacher called her class, Susie marched to the front with the others. They stood side by side, with the tips of their shoes in a straight line, and solemnly answered the teacher's questions, one student at a time. When class was over, the students put away their books and slates, folded their arms, and waited for dismissal.

But Susie was always happiest when she was home. There she could walk beside her father as he plowed the rich black soil, or sew and cook and talk quietly with her mother and sisters, or sit contentedly by the wood fire and peel fat orange pumpkins in spirals like an apple. And when thunder rolled across the sky and lightning ripped open the rain clouds, she was glad to be with her family, warm and dry and together.

When there was sickness, Susie would watch the white government doctor use his white medicine. The white medicine didn't always work, and even if it did, most Omahas preferred to call the Omaha medicine men and women. Susie learned how the Omaha doctors treated sick or injured patients with herbs, such as sage, and sweat baths and songs and prayers to Wakon'da.

In 1875, when Susie was ten, her sister Susette returned home from Elizabeth, New Jersey, where she had been at school at the Elizabeth Institute for Young Ladies. One of Susette's teachers at the mission school had arranged for this chance for her, and Susette had done very well. She had not only studied academic subjects, but she had also learned how to live confidently in the white world.

Susette became a teacher at the Omaha Agency school. She found a little brown house close to the school, and the four sisters moved in together. Susette "supported the little household," Susie said later, and the rest of them kept the house clean and comfortable. In the evenings, Susette would read out loud by the fire while Susie and Rosalie and Marguerite sewed. Susie tried and tried to make neat stitches, but she never learned to sew very well and finally gave up. She would much rather cook, she decided.

Susie watched her oldest sister attentively. She

The bones of thousands of buffalo. By the mid-1870s, without the buffalo, the Omahas faced the constant problem of never having enough meat. To make matters worse, grasshoppers destroyed the Omahas' crops in 1876.

helped Susette arrange her new classroom. She learned to play the organ when Susette bought one for her class. And she listened carefully to Susette and Iron Eye when they discussed the difficulty of being an Indian in a world that was no longer theirs, the difficulty of being *in between* worlds.

Being together helped Susie and her family when times were hard, and hard times and confusion were still plentiful on the reservation. Many of the Omahas were often sick now, as a result of eating new kinds of food, of being exposed to new germs, and of living a softer and less vigorous life. The government doctor, Susie noticed, was not well skilled in treating the Indians. But even worse, it often seemed that he didn't care whether he helped them or not. This indifference puzzled and disturbed her.

After several very hungry years, the Omahas began to realize that farming *was* the only way to survive. But now they were greatly troubled by reports that their friends and neighbors the Ponca Indians were to be taken to "Indian Territory" (later Oklahoma), whether they liked it or not. Naturally the Omahas feared the same fate. Why build and plow and plant, they asked, when at any time they, too, might be removed from their land? But if crops were not planted, the only solution was to hunt—and that no longer worked, either. The proud Omahas were deeply insulted to have to be given food by the government agent. And to add to the confusion, most white Indian agents had very little understanding of Indian beliefs and manners and saw no reason to understand them, anyway.

Eighteen seventy-six was a momentous year. It was the one-hundredth anniversary of the Declaration of Independence ("All men are created equal . . ."). In Philadelphia the Centennial Exposition was packed with excited visitors getting their first look at the typewriter and the telegraph, among other marvelous inventions. On the Little Big Horn River, Lt. Col. Custer and his troops were killed by a force of Cheyenne and Sioux in what came to be known as Custer's Last Stand.

Actually it was the *Indians'* last stand. The very next year, all the Plains Indians had given up (except Sitting Bull, who fled to Canada) and were taken to reservations. In the Northwest, the Nez Perce had one more year of flight before Chief Joseph said, "I will fight no more forever." And in Nebraska, the Omahas, who could no longer live in the traditional Indian ways, struggled to live in the new and puzzling ways of the white man.

Meanwhile Susie LaFlesche was growing up. She loved her family, her pony, the prairie, and her people. She didn't know what to do with all these loves, so "what to do" lay there and simmered in her mind. She could see plenty of problems to solve, though. Susie knew that if she wanted to help her people, she must succeed in the white world. The only question was how.

III
Out East

In the fall of 1879, Susan's prairie childhood came to an end. Susan, fourteen, and her sister Marguerite, seventeen, now had their turn to go to the Elizabeth Institute for Young Ladies. Their schooling was paid for, as Susette's had been, by friends of the institute. Susan was eager to learn everything about the strange world east of the prairie.

The roaring, rattling iron horse took Susan and her sister away from the world they knew and let them out, several days later, in New Jersey. As people rushed to get off the train, Susan stood up on shaky legs. She took a deep breath and brushed the coal soot from her face. Then she straightened her hat and her back and picked up her bag, and she and Marguerite walked forward bravely, as proud Omaha girls should.

Susan wasn't feeling quite so brave on the inside, however, and she was relieved to hear someone calling

Susan (standing) and her sister Marguerite (with book) in about 1879

their names. The ladies who had come to meet them had had no trouble finding the two young Indian girls in the crowd of white people milling about the platform. Susan held out her hand with a wide smile and greeted their new friends.

Soon they were on their way to the institute, seated in a horse-drawn trolley car. Susan tried to keep her mind on the conversation as she gazed with wide eyes at the tall buildings and houses lining the busy streets. There were so *many* buildings, so *many* horses pulling buggies of all sizes, and so *many* people dashing in all directions. Even after all Susette had told her, Susan hadn't imagined the white world could be so crowded, so noisy, so . . . foreign.

For three years, Susan and her sister studied math, reading, writing, spelling, composition, philosophy, physiology, and literature. They learned to live as white people did, and Susan's good English quickly became excellent English. Susan and Marguerite didn't have money for train fare home during summer vacations, but they did feel a little less homesick when other students at the institute invited them to visit their homes.

Once, Susette came to see them while she was on a speaking tour with Francis and Standing Bear of the Poncas, asking white audiences for fair treatment of Indians. Susan was proud of Susette's ability to help white people see the problems Indians were facing.

Susan and Marguerite finished their classes at the institute in 1882 and bid good-bye to their teachers and friends. Although Susan was very grateful for all she had learned and all the friends she had made, the train they rode home couldn't go fast enough for her.

With a whoop of joy, Susan jumped down the metal steps when the puffing train stopped at the little station on the reservation. Her father was waiting. He piled the girls' trunks into the wagon, and Susan and Marguerite leaped onto the wooden seat. The horses trotted off, flicking their ears at all the chatter and laughter coming from the old wagon behind them.

At last they were home. Susan packed her stiff leather shoes away, put on her soft moccasins, and let her thick braids hang down her back. She played with her sister Rosalie's children and galloped her pony over the grassy hills. As Susan rode over the reservation, she saw more than one hundred new wooden houses built on small farms. She was glad that so many of the Omahas were following her father's example.

But when Susan got off her pony and talked with the men and women she had known all her life, she learned they were very discouraged. They were trying to learn new ways of living and working, but it was hard to cross from one world to another without falling into a chasm. They needed a bridge by which they could cross. Iron Eye was discouraged at times, too, and he was angered when the government seemed to have one rule for them one day and a different rule the next. Susan pondered these problems as she walked her tired pony past worn tipis and crumbling earth lodges.

Susan was always busy. She taught at the old mission school on the bluff, which had reopened in 1879, and helped her mother at home. She also helped the reservation doctor by caring for an anthropologist who was staying on the reservation. The anthropologist, Alice Fletcher, had come to Nebraska in 1881 to study the Plains Indians, and she had insisted on living in a canvas tent (her tipi) so she could better understand Indian ways. By 1883, however, after being out in too many cold thunderstorms in too many drenched tents, she became so sick that she needed a nurse. Susan stepped right in to help. It felt easy and natural to her. She thought again about all the sickness among the Omahas and saw again the indifference of the white government doctor. Perhaps *she* could learn the skills needed to help her people become strong and healthy and happy again. As she considered this idea, Susan felt little leaps of excitement stirring inside, like soft, swift thumps on an Indian drum.

In the fall of 1884, Susan and Marguerite went by train to Hampton, Virginia. They had both been awarded scholarships to attend the Hampton Institute. The institute, which had opened in 1868 as a school for newly freed blacks, had begun accepting Indian students in 1879. Indian boys had come to Hampton that first year wearing their blankets, with soft moccasins on their feet. They wore their long black hair hanging loose or in braids. But they had come to learn how to live in the white world. Soon their long hair was cut short, their blankets were replaced by suits and ties, and their feet were squeezed into heavy leather shoes.

When Susan and Marguerite arrived, they were greeted warmly by a mixture of white teachers, black students, and Indian students. Susan and Marguerite moved right into Winona Hall—the new dormitory for Indian girls—unpacked their few dresses, and got ready for another new experience.

The day began early at Hampton. Susan jumped out of bed at five o'clock, scrubbed hurriedly at the wash-basin, and fastened her long braids into a large bun at the nape of her neck. Then she put on her dark high-buttoned uniform and pulled on her stiff high-buttoned shoes, and she was ready for the day. She went to classes in the morning and worked in the laundry or sewing room in the afternoon. She also swept and dusted the corridors and workrooms, and tutored students who needed extra help. The boys went to classes in the morning and learned farming in the afternoon.

Every morning Susan slid into the seat of her desk in the wood-paneled classroom and lifted the desk lid to put her books neatly inside. Her desk, like all the others, was made of wood and fancy scrolled cast iron and was attached to the chair in front. She waited, notebook and pen and ink ready, for the teacher to begin his lecture. And she carefully avoided looking at the boys who were, amazingly, in the same classroom.

At first Susan was shocked to see boys and girls in the same classroom, because an Omaha girl was never

A sewing class in Winona Hall

to be left alone with a boy. She was supposed to be always in the care of her mother, aunt, or grandmother. Omaha good manners said that a young man and young woman could meet "accidentally," but certainly never on purpose.

Hampton was teaching a new way of life.

Susan got over her surprise very quickly and was soon writing home about the wonderful Saturday night socials. Winona Hall took the place of the Indian girls' homes and the teachers took the place of the girls' families. This arrangement was considered safe enough that the boys could come for Saturday and Sunday evening dinner, and twice a month they could stay for "good fun" after dinner. Susan wrote home happily that they had "games, conversation, marching, and literary and musical exercises."

Susan soon found several young men she liked very much, and she began to see one in particular—a Sioux named Thomas Ikinicapi. She called him T.I. Susan's plans did not include marriage, however, and she told T.I. kindly that friendship was all there could ever be between them.

Susan's sweet, gentle nature brought her many friends. She did well in her classwork, too, and it was at Hampton that she decided what to do with her life. She decided to become a doctor, a doctor for her people. It didn't matter to her that at that time even few white women were doctors. Susan knew her people had to learn to stay healthy in wooden houses, on a reservation, in a new world. "The home is the foundation of all things for the Indian," she said, "and my work I hope will be chiefly in the homes of my people."

Susan's desire to become a doctor had grown slowly but steadily. It had begun during her childhood when she had first seen how little the white government doctor helped the Omahas. Her conviction had increased as she grew older and saw her people continue to sicken and die, sometimes without even trying to call the white doctor. Then at Hampton, Susan met Dr. Martha M. Waldron, the school doctor. Dr. Waldron was one of the country's few women doctors. Susan's conviction grew even stronger.

In the spring of her second year at Hampton, Susan

applied for admission to Women's Medical College, in Philadelphia, the same college Dr. Waldron had attended. Then she waited nervously to hear whether she would be accepted.

Susan's recommendations were glowing, but still she worried. Would the medical school accept her, an Indian? And how would she pay her tuition if they did? Then she heard from the school. She was accepted as a medical student at Women's Medical College for the fall term.

As she recovered from her excitement, Susan and her teachers worked on the problem of money. The women of the Connecticut Indian Association offered to provide complete financial support for Susan. The levelheaded Susan was overwhelmed and wrote from Hampton to thank all her "many mothers" who were going to help. "I cannot tell you how thankful I feel to all of you, and how glad to think that through me you will be helping so many people. I can scarcely realize that my desire is granted," she wrote, jubilantly.

In May 1886, Susan graduated from Hampton as the class salutatorian, the student who gives the opening speech. (Marguerite had returned to the reservation in 1885 and did not graduate until the next year.)

Susan was very disappointed that her parents could not be at the graduation. But Alice Fletcher, the woman Susan had helped nurse back to health in 1883, came from Washington, D.C., to watch the ceremony. Accompanying her was a large group of people who were interested in helping Indians succeed in a new

Francis and Susette
LaFlesche in Wash-
ington, D.C., during
a lecture tour to ac-
quaint people with
Indian problems

way of life. There were over one thousand people in
the audience that day.

Susan wore a simple striped dress—her best dress—
and everyone said she looked very neat and pretty.
Nobody knew how frightened she was when she walked
forward to give her speech. She clenched her cold
hands to stop them from trembling and looked out
onto more people than there were in her entire village.
Then she began. Susan's speech was entitled "My
Childhood and Womanhood," and the audience listened
intently to her soft, firm voice.

(Above) Susan (center) dressed in traditional Indian clothing for a graduation presentation. To the right is Charles Picotte, who later married Marguerite. (Below) Hampton class of 1886. Susan is in the second row.

Susan first told the audience about her happy childhood and warm family life. "But life changes," she said. "We have to prepare our people to live in the white man's way, to use the white man's books, and his laws." Susan also reminded her listeners that although white people might have attained a high level of civilization, how many years had it taken them? She explained that Indians had only begun to try this new way and must be given time, too. For herself, Susan said, "The shores of success can only be reached by crossing the bridge of faith, and I shall try hard."

When she finished, the audience clapped long and hard. But there was more to come. Susan was called forward again and given a gold medal for her excellent work. This time she was so overcome that she couldn't look at the audience. She couldn't even look at General Cutcheon, who presented the gold medal to her. As she stood, shy and silent, he said, "This is for the excellence with which you have laid a foundation. I know you already appreciate how great a thing it is to be one of the first women of your race to go out to lay its foundations." Susan heard his words as if in a dream. "You must build *yourself* into their foundations," General Cutcheon went on. "I charge you to regard it as your duty to live for your people."

Susan thanked him in a whisper. As she returned to her chair, she felt more sure than ever that she had made the right decision.

IV
Medical School

Susan tried to appear calm as she stepped off the train in Philadelphia, but her heart pounded like a running horse and her hands shook as she collected her bags and greeted the two women who had come to meet her. It was October 1886, and again Susan was going to a new school, to a new city, to a new life, but this time she was alone. Marguerite was not with her, Susette had not attended this school, and there would be no other Indians there.

Susan felt a little sick, very tired, and exceedingly worried about how well she would do. All the other students, she feared, would have been educated at large universities. They might be better prepared than she. But she had so many dreams for her people—she *could not* fail.

The street outside the massive red brick train station was lined with other imposing brick buildings.

Wanamaker's Department Store in about 1885

Wanamaker's Department Store, next to the station, looked like a castle, with flags flying from its towers and spires. As the horsecab drove Susan to the rooming house, she marveled at the crowds of people rushing here and there and at the clouds of black smoke billowing from the riverfront iron and steel factories. Her ears rang with the clang of bells, the clamor of voices, and the clatter of iron-shod hooves on the cobblestones. She clasped her shaking hands together tightly and reminded herself that she was here to become a doctor. She *would* become a doctor.

As soon as she stepped into her new home and met Mrs. Smith, the landlady, Susan felt better. Mrs. Smith greeted her warmly and showed her to the room that she would share with another young woman. Susan liked her roommate immediately, although at first she was alarmed to see that the other young woman's dresses were all silk and lace. By the time Susan had hung her simple dresses in the wardrobe and arranged her things on the washstand, the two women were laughing like old friends. And by the time dinner was over, Susan felt welcomed and at ease with all the other boarders.

The next day, Susan walked up to the college to register, along with the other new students and again she felt warmly welcomed. In fact she was so warmly welcomed that it was a little embarrassing. The dean of the college kissed Susan, and only Susan, in front of everybody and said how proud she was of Susan's heritage. (Perhaps white people were still somewhat surprised that an Indian woman would be as civilized and educated as a white woman.)

That evening Susan was dreadfully homesick. She sat down to write to her family about her trip, her boardinghouse, and her welcome, but she ended up saying she wished she were back home again. As she was about to start crying, Susan stopped to look around her half of the tidy little room. She had made it homelike and cheerful by hanging her flowered hats and bead necklaces and pictures and cards on the walls. So she added in her letter that her room and roommate were quite cheery, and she began to feel better immediately.

The very next day, Susan was too busy to be home-sick anymore. Classes began. Every morning Susan walked past rows of identical brick houses to the large brick medical school. In the lecture room, she took out her sharpened pencils, opened her notebook on her lap, and waited with thirty-five other women for the lesson (chemistry, anatomy, physiology, histology, general therapeutics, or obstetrics) to begin.

By November Susan and her classmates were ready to cut up human bodies. They had already memorized the names of every groove, depression, and hole in every bone, and now they took up their knives. The dissection class was in the evening, after dinner. But the well-brought-up young ladies didn't shrink from their task, nor from the smell of the formaldehyde—the chemical that preserved the dead bodies—that clung to every living thing in the dissection room. In fact, Susan wrote home cheerfully, they laughed and talked just as much there as anywhere else.

Of course when it came time to work, the women were very serious. Six students leaned over each life-less body, two at the head, two at the chest, and two at the abdomen and legs. Carefully, following their instructor's lead, each student inserted her razor-sharp knife and cautiously peeled back the yellowed skin. The next step was to lift off the tissue that covered the muscles. Then each muscle was thoroughly dissected so the arteries and veins and nerves could be examined. Susan was fascinated by the design of the human body, and she thought the class was simply splendid.

Susan read and studied from early morning to late night. Mrs. Smith's boardinghouse was peaceful, very peaceful, and although Susan had not liked this at first, because it seemed too quiet for her playful nature, now she was grateful. She wanted no shrieks or laughs or thumps to distract her.

When Christmas came, Susan put aside her books and went to Hampton to visit her old friends and Marguerite. Her former boyfriend, T.I., was there, too, and he was more attentive than ever. Susan's resolve was quite torn by his seriousness, and she confided in a friend that T.I. had a place in her heart no one else had. She had to remind herself sternly that her life was already mapped out, because she had decided long ago that she would be a doctor who lived only for her people.

Susan stuck with her resolve, but when she left, she could not look at T.I. because it hurt too much. Later she learned that he was as upset as she was.

She wrote home about her wonderful Christmas gifts (a handkerchief and a card and a calendar and a ring) and about the new fashion she was wearing (a bustle) and about how terribly much she missed home at Christmastime.

But Susan's irrepressible spirits couldn't lay low for long. Soon her familiar giggle filled the dining room, the dissection room, and the lecture hall. And just in time, too.

The time had come for Susan's class to observe its first operation. The women sat in six circular rows,

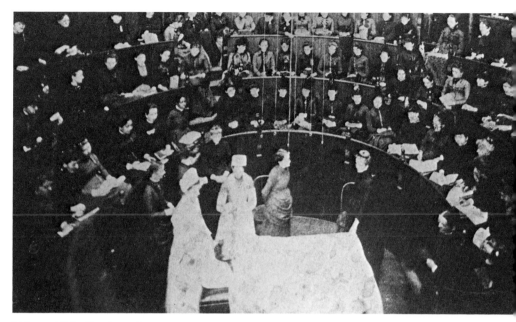

(Above) Medical students preparing to observe an operation. (Below) Medical students working in the laboratory. Both photographs were taken at Women's Medical College of Pennsylvania in about 1890.

each row higher toward the ceiling, surrounding the small operating area. A men's class had been invited to watch as well, and they sat very importantly right down in front. The men didn't so much as look at the delicate young women, who were sure to scream and faint when the operation started. The room was lit as well as possible by gas jets and a large skylight directly over the operating table. With her notebook open on the railing in front of her, Susan took notes furiously as the doctors explained the case.

The head surgeon had just made his first cut when there was a commotion in the front row. The surgeon stopped. The delicate young women leaned forward and peered down with concern. To their astonishment, one of the young men had fainted. Susan and the other women bit their lips to keep from laughing as the unfortunate man was carried out by two red-faced classmates. The surgeon continued his cutting, the women continued taking notes, and the men's class sat in silence.

We were not even *thinking* of fainting, Susan wrote home later with delicious satisfaction.

In March 1887, Susan had exams. After passing the dreaded chemistry exam, the whole class celebrated with a candy pull. After passing anatomy, Susan spent the day with a friend. They walked along the Schuylkill River, gathered pinecones, and sat on a rock in Fairmount Park and talked. Then they went back home and had a feast of brown bread and butter, peaches and cream, cookies, and coffee.

   Although Susan had anatomy and bones and veins constantly on her mind, she also kept up with the news from home.   In 1887 there was very important news indeed.   Susan learned that she, and every Omaha, had become a citizen of the United States on February 7. (Not until 1924 did *all* Indians—the first people of America—become citizens.)

   Susan, now an American citizen, continued her work as before.   And during her vacation breaks, she had time to explore Philadelphia with her friends.   The city was in full literary and artistic bloom, with a club for every possible interest, from boating to zoology. Susan attended concerts and plays.   She went to museums and art galleries.   She explored the Academy of Natural Sciences, with its rows of stuffed birds and colossal skeletons.   She visited Independence Hall, where she was stared at with such curiosity that she and her friends left, in giggles.   And she strolled past row after row of red brick houses with green and white shutters and white marble steps.

   Susan was invited into some of the finest homes in Philadelphia.   She saw homes that were fragrant with the pleasant smell of red roses and wax and filled with beautiful carpets and starched curtains and polished furniture.   She saw Quaker ladies in their soft gray dresses.   She saw elderly gentlemen who used ear trumpets, the better to hear.

   Once she stayed overnight in one of these fine homes. She marveled at the ivory comb and brush set on the washstand in the great big bedroom she had all to herself. But that was nothing compared to breakfast the next morning. After a first course of oranges, servants brought in finger bowls. Susan carefully watched the others at the table before she dipped her fingers in the warm water as they did. After that there were kidneys and gravy, potatoes, bread and butter, and coffee in a great silver urn. Susan enjoyed the meal immensely, but she sighed as she thought of the people at home who didn't have good food like this, who sometimes didn't even have *enough* food.

Susan knew that many opportunities not available to other Indians came her way because of her friendships at the college and because of her friendship with Alice Fletcher. But she also found that many Philadelphians were genuinely concerned about the problems Indians faced and wanted to help *all* Indians. She watched closely and learned thoroughly these new ways of living so that she could teach them to those at home on the reservation.

Often Susan's heart sank as she read letters from home telling of the confusion and misery and sorrow her people endured every single day as they tried to adjust to the routine of reservation life. Many did not adjust, they simply gave up.

She knew that her half-brother, Francis, was diligently writing down every traditional Omaha ceremony and song before all those who knew them died. Watching the old, old men perform these ceremonies, Francis told her, was like watching the last dying embers of a fire fade and flicker out. Susan's head ached with impatience. Every day she was one day closer to knowing all the skills she needed to help her people, but she wasn't ready yet.

As busy as she was, Susan never forgot the people who had helped her and the reason she was at medical school. She visited homes for Indian children, and at church she sang hymns for her white friends in the Omaha language. When she spoke at ladies' meetings, she suggested the ladies send illustrated magazines, such as *Godey's Lady's Book* and *Harper's*, to the women back home to show them how white women dressed. (But apparently the women back home didn't find them useful.) Susan described for the Philadelphia Indian Association how dreadful it was for her people not to have proper care. And she told them about a dream she had that someday there would be a hospital on the reservation.

Susan was so busy that her once-neat room was covered with piles of papers, and she couldn't even find the letters she wanted to answer when she found the time to answer them. Her days were so filled with classes that a spare hour for study was "like a little vacation." But she was very happy. "I have so much to be thankful for," she wrote to a friend, "it almost takes my breath away."

With spring 1888 came her second-year exams in anatomy, chemistry, and physiology, and Susan needed a sharp knife, for cutting up a body, in addition to pen and paper. Her heart beat quickly, but her hands did not tremble, and Susan passed all her exams. One more year and she would graduate, if she could keep up her good work.

That summer Susan went home to the reservation for the first time in two years. Both her mother and father had been sick and were getting old, so she had plenty of farm work to do. "I can tell you one thing," she wrote to a friend, "and that is that a Western woman has to know how to do everything that a man does, besides her own work, for she has to be ready for any emergency."

Susan put up the hay, cooked, sewed, measured for a new fence, and drove the wagon about twenty-five miles a day to visit people who were just getting over a serious measles epidemic. Every night when she fell into bed, her satisfaction at finally helping her people was thoroughly mixed with the frustration of seeing how much there was to do and with having to leave again all too soon.

In September, after Susan returned to Philadelphia, her father died. She grieved because she missed him and because he had not lived to see her return to the Omahas as a doctor.

The months flew by like fast-flung arrows, and in January 1889, she wrote with alarm to a friend at Hampton, "I feel as if I don't know a single thing and my degree is only 6 weeks off—at least I hope it is."

Still, when she was asked to portray Pocahontas at an "entertainment" at the Philadelphia Academy of Fine Arts, Susan found the time. She immediately asked Miss Folsom, one of her favorite teachers at

Hampton Institute, if she could wear the elegant white buckskin dress, covered with beads and wampum, that Hampton owned. The soft, supple dress was so valuable it was kept in a showcase, but it was sent to Susan without question. On the evening of the performance, the audience applauded loudly for Pocahontas and her beautiful dress—a dress that represented a time that was gone forever and a heritage that even the most concerned white person in Philadelphia could never understand.

And then she was finished. In March 1889, Susan, who had worried so much about being able to keep up with the other students, graduated in the top half of her class of thirty-six women. She wrote one word to Hampton: "Passed!!!!!"

Susan graduated with a turbulent mixture of pride and sadness, for she missed her wise, thoughtful father terribly. "You don't know how it felt to receive my degree," she wrote to Miss Folsom, "and not to have him there." But Susan knew her father had always been proud of what she accomplished and of her steady determination to help their people.

So at last, in late 1889, twenty-four-year-old Dr. Susan LaFlesche returned to the prairie.

V
A Doctor for Her People

It was a good thing Susan loved to ride. She had 1,244 patients to see, and they lived in tipis and earth lodges and frame houses all over the Omaha Reservation. Susan started as the school doctor, but soon she was made government doctor for the whole reservation because her people trusted her more than the agency doctor.

Often the only way to get over the roller coaster hills and rugged roads—if there even was a road—was on horseback. And Susan often had to ride fast to reach her patients in time. No matter how carefully she packed her bottles and thermometers in her saddlebags, she found broken bottles and broken thermometers when she opened her bags. Susan hadn't yet solved this problem when winter swept in, as if on the silent wings of the great snowy owl.

It was an ordinary prairie winter, with bitter cold

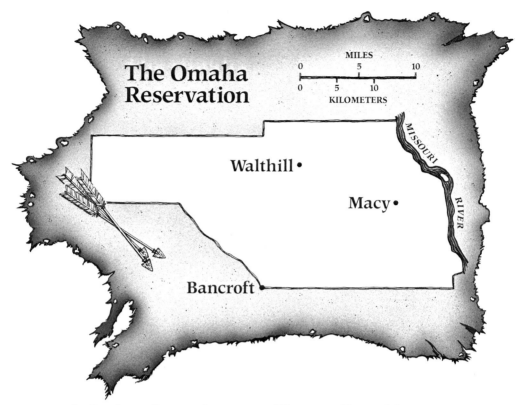

The Omaha Reservation

winds that drove the snow like needles, skies as gray as ashes, deep and dangerous snowdrifts, and long, black nights. And people still got sick. In fact more people were sick in the winter. So Susan rode, day or night, through the drifting snow. Even though she wrapped up as warmly as she could in a heavy coat and thick shawls and mufflers, the howling wind cut through to her ears and face until she felt like ice. Unwrapping and thawing out beside a patient's small cookstove was almost as painful as the freezing. But when people were sick or dying, the doctor had to go, and the doctor went, all winter long.

The next year, 1890, Susan bought a covered carriage

and a team of horses. This was better. The bottles and thermometers didn't break as often, and Susan didn't freeze as often. Still, there were many places where only a horse and rider could get through, especially in the winter snows, when the drifts buried pathways and hid treacherous gullies, or in the pouring rain, when the dirt roads turned to mud pudding.

Of course Susan didn't *always* have to go to her patients. Sometimes they came to her. Her office and home was a long one-story building at the Omaha Agency school in Macy. She was the doctor for all the children at the school, too. Susan made her office a warm and welcoming place for children and adults by filling it with plants, games, books, and magazines. Most welcoming of all was Susan herself. Her kind smile and gentle, sympathetic voice calmed the fears of her patients and gave them hope. And, unlike the past government doctors, she spoke their language.

Right from the beginning, Susan was not only the doctor for her people, but their adviser as well. She reminded everyone of the traditional Omaha question, How can we better ourselves? and tried to keep it foremost in their minds, as well as in her own. She knew as well as any Indian how hard it was to be born in one culture and become part of another culture. Susan meant to be the bridge on which her people would cross to that new way of life.

Susan saw her mother and Marguerite and Rosalie almost every day. Marguerite taught at the government school, so she and Susan were frequently together.

Susan's sister Rosalie. Rosalie LaFlesche married Edward Farley, who first came to the reservation as an organ salesman and sold Susette an organ for her classroom.

Susan's mother and Rosalie both lived on the reservation, within a pleasant buggy drive of the school.

Susan liked some of the customs she had seen back East so much that she wanted to introduce them to the Omahas. She and Marguerite decided to show the Omahas how to have a church wedding. Susan persuaded a young Omaha man and woman to have their wedding at the Blackbird Hills Presbyterian Church, instead of in the Omaha way. It was probably the first church wedding on the reservation and the first most of the Omahas had ever seen. On the big day, the church was crowded with curious, interested Omahas, most wearing "citizens' clothing" (white people's clothing) and a few in their blankets. Marguerite sat at the organ, ready to play. Susan did her best to explain the new ceremony, but it turned out very badly.

When the minister asked the young couple to join hands, they refused, because this was considered bad manners by the Omahas. After the couple was pronounced husband and wife, they didn't know what to do, so they just stood there. Finally the minister said, "You may go," and they turned, walked down two different aisles, and sat down on opposite sides of the church. It was all so terribly embarrassing that few Omahas tried a church wedding for years after. It was much easier for the man, after a suitable gift of horses to the woman's father, to simply put his blanket over the shoulders of his intended wife so everyone would know she was in his keeping.

This experience was discouraging for Susan, and she felt terrible about the results, which reminded her once again how difficult it was for her people to change from one way of life to another.

And not far away, at Wounded Knee Creek in South Dakota, the Plains Indians' way ended finally and forever in December 1890. A group of Sioux Indians were found guilty of dancing the Ghost Dance, which they believed would bring back the buffalo and remove the white man. There, in their peaceful camp on the Pine Ridge Reservation, more than 250 Sioux men, women, boys, girls, and babies were killed by 500 soldiers and left in the snow.

Despite the shock of this massacre, despite the actions of some white people, Susan saw only one way to direct her people, and that was the white way. There *was* no other way now. And the Omahas were making

Sioux Indians performing the Ghost Dance. At one time, each of these people would have been wearing a buffalo robe, which was the necessary everyday — as well as ceremonial — piece of clothing for the Plains Indians. When the buffalo became scarce, the robe was replaced by a blanket, which served the same purpose.

some progress, Susan believed, except for one dreadful problem. Alcohol.

In the days when Susan's father was chief, he had organized a police force to punish drinkers severely. The Omaha police wore dark green uniforms, made by Susan's mother, with a star badge. Their duty was to arrest and punish any Omaha who was drunk. Then the Omahas had been proud to say that no Omaha was ever seen drunk. But Susan found that they could not say that now.

In 1888, when the Omahas could vote for the first

time, the alcohol problem had returned. Immediately, and illegally, white men had come to the reservation and bought the Omaha votes with alcohol. "They even gave whiskey to the little children," Susan said later, her dark eyes blazing with fury.

Susan had returned home just in time. At the very next election after her return, the Omahas were to vote on a prohibition law that would make alcohol illegal on the reservation. A white man who made money by selling alcohol rode through the reservation giving out free dinners and "helpful" voting tickets to people who could not read. The tickets said "Against Prohibition," but people who wanted to vote against alcohol started off to vote with these tickets. Luckily Susan saw a ticket just in time. She jumped on her horse and followed the trail of the dinners and tickets. By riding fast, she had time to explain to the people before they voted that "Against Prohibition" really meant *for* alcohol. Prohibition won, but alcohol was sold illegally anyway.

Despite her anger over the alcohol problem, Susan was very happy. She was up early, doctoring, advising, translating, and encouraging. She started a reading room with newspapers and scrapbooks and games, and she helped with a sewing circle, a night school, Sunday school and church, and clubs for young people. Her dream of a hospital on the reservation was still a dream, a hope for the future. But another dream had come true—Susan was a bridge for her people between old and new ways.

That winter Susan wrapped herself in still thicker shawls and mufflers and rode through the snow to see more than 640 patients. She went back to see some patients every two or three days, and still other patients came to see her. It was Susan's third winter as the Omahas' only doctor, and there was more sickness than one doctor on horseback could take care of. But there *was* only one doctor.

Susan would start out by seven or eight o'clock in the morning, stop at home for lunch, and finally return at ten o'clock at night, with her horses worn out. As before, blizzards and storms whipped through her wraps, and often her ears and face felt frozen and brittle right down to the bones. Sometimes Susan drooped with weariness and wanted only to stay inside by her own warm fire. But each time a desperate father or mother struggled through the snow to her door, she would snatch up her medical bag and hurry out. After treating each patient, Susan would once again carefully explain ways to stay well in closed wooden houses and once again show the women how to cook now that they no longer had fresh game. Her goal was to prevent sickness, not just to give medicine after sickness came. Susan's fingers might tremble from cold and exhaustion, but her firm chin and steady eyes did not.

One bitterly cold night, Susan learned that a young girl was dying. When she got to the one-room house, she found the girl on the only bed, in one neat corner of the room. The family had two chairs, one table, the one bed, and no food. Susan went back to her office and loaded a sled with milk, eggs, and meat. She returned to the family and cooked them their first meal in four days. The girl lived for two more weeks, and Susan visited the family every day, each time taking them food and cooking it for them.

That winter Susan's hopes were raised by the news that a hospital would finally be built on the reservation. With great excitement, she wrote to the *Indians' Friend* newspaper, "When the new hospital is built in the spring, then we will rejoice, for it will give the Indians a chance to receive proper care during sickness." But there wasn't enough money, and to Susan's great disappointment, the expected hospital was not built.

Spring came at last, and as the wildflowers bloomed on the prairie, Susan began to feel more energetic. It was a good thing, because her understanding and common sense were needed more than ever. The Omahas' traditional tribal rules and structure had disappeared since chiefs were abolished and the Omahas had become United States citizens. Now they were to follow rules sent from Washington. The white Indian agent was supposed to see that all the rules were followed and that all the correct forms were filled out. As an interpreter of both language and beliefs, Susan tried to explain Omaha needs to the white agent and white rules to the Omahas.

Despite the government's concern about rules, some white people were breaking them. Whites were using Indian land for cattle grazing without permission. But that wasn't the worst problem. The most serious problem was still alcohol, which whites were all too happy to sell to Indians. Unfortunately there was no medicine in Susan's medical bag to cure this problem.

Susan added little lectures about the evils of drinking to her house calls. She explained patiently, in Omaha, that the way to better oneself was to avoid drinking alcohol. She complained impatiently and furiously, in English, to the whites who sold the alcohol. But the white men just laughed at the young Indian doctor with the angry brown eyes, and they continued selling alcohol as fast as they could. And many of the Indians, who were worn down with bitter discouragement and grief over the loss of their land and their buffalo and their traditions, found easy escape in alcohol, for only a few found the transition to new ways as smooth as Susan tried to make it.

A year later, in 1893, the alcohol problem was worse than ever. Susan was exasperated and outraged. In July she wrote in her report to the Indian Association that the Indians got whiskey from whites as easily as water. The Indians could not make any progress with this drink among them, she said hotly. "I hope you can somehow help us." There was no real chief, no one in charge. Susan said that even little children were drunk in the streets and no life was safe. Now, besides being a doctor and teacher and translator and adviser, Susan became a counselor for those who tried to stop drinking and a nettle to those who didn't.

But Susan had also been very sick with earaches

Back in 1853, Chief Big Elk of the Omahas had warned his people about the coming flood of white people. Soon, he said, the animals that Wakon'da had given them for sustenance would disappear beneath that flood to return no more.

In 1850 there were fifty *million* buffalo. In 1883 there were fifty.

and headaches and backaches from being out day and night for four years, shaking with cold in the winter and burning with heat in the summer. She was only twenty-eight years old, but she felt as fragile and withered as an autumn leaf. Now when desperate people came to see her, her legs could not even carry her to the door.

Susan could hardly believe that her whole life's dream seemed to be ending. She had only begun! All summer she fought against her own sickness, against the alcoholism that spread like a prairie grass fire through the Omahas, and for her patients' good health. But the battle was too great.

In October 1893, Susan sat at her desk and slowly dipped her pen into the inkwell. Her hand shook, and she put the pen down. Then she turned up the wick in her lamp, picked up the pen again, and began to write to the U.S. Department of the Interior. Sadly, she wrote, she would have to give up her job as government doctor.

When the editor of the Hampton Institute newspaper heard of Susan's decision, he wrote, "Dr. Susan LaFlesche, who has been doctor to the whole Omaha tribe for nearly five years—doing more than three strong men ought to do—finally had to resign."

VI
A Family of Her Own

After a few months' rest, Susan's earaches and tiredness began to fade, and she began to think about what she should do next. Certainly she could never abandon her people and her family and live in a turbulent, noisy city full of white people. Definitely she had to help her people keep asking, How can we better ourselves? Possibly she could continue her dream of doctoring and teaching her people, even though she wasn't strong enough to go back to the way she had lived before.

What she did next surprised everyone. Susan had always said that she would never marry, because it was her life's plan to be a doctor and to devote her whole life to her people. Then, in the summer of 1894, Susan married Henry Picotte—a charming man with a good sense of humor, a Sioux Indian who was, Susan said, "utterly unlike" herself.

Susan's friends and family couldn't understand it at all. Even Marguerite didn't understand it, and she had been married to Henry's brother Charles, who had died in 1892. People weren't sure it was such a good idea, either, but that didn't stop Susan. Perhaps she realized that she could be a doctor and be married, too. Perhaps she wanted to have children, as other women did. And perhaps she just couldn't live without Henry Picotte.

In 1895 Susan was very sick again, with the same pain in her ears and head. She was so sick that Rosalie wrote to Francis that the family had almost given up hope that Susan would live. Susan's mother was in despair. But, happily, Susan's dark eyes began to sparkle again. Soon she could sit up and brush her thick hair and pile it on top of her head. When she was finally well, she and Henry moved to Bancroft, Nebraska, another town on the reservation. They planted lilies and lilacs and peonies all around their new house. They had a large orchard and garden with plums, cherries, apples, apricots, strawberries, asparagus, and more. And before long, they had a baby boy, Caryl.

Best of all, Susan returned to her life's dream. In 1896 she wrote Miss Folsom that she was practicing medicine again, while her husband took care of the new baby. "Henry worships the baby," she wrote. "They are the greatest of friends." Susan left a lantern in the window every night so people in need could quickly find her, and she always went where she was needed, whether the patient was Indian or white.

Susan (left) and Marguerite with their husbands, Henry Picotte, (seated) and Walter Diddock, in the doorway of Mary Gale LaFlesche's house. Susan is only in her early thirties in this picture.

(Many white families lived on Omaha land, renting it from the Omaha owners at four cents to twenty-five cents an acre.) By this time, there were two other doctors close by, doing what Susan had tried to do by herself for five years, and these men often called on her for help and advice.

Again in 1897, Susan nearly died. Somehow she never completely got over the earaches and backaches that had started on her winter rides when she first became a doctor. This time, worried Omahas and whites (Swedes, Danes, Irish, and Germans) from all over the reservation came to help and encourage her, bringing food and flowers and concern. In the past, Susan had often felt sad and discouraged when she tried to solve the problems she saw every day, and she had thought that perhaps her work was for nothing. Now, for the first time, Susan realized how much her people needed and appreciated her. That December, when she was better, she wrote to Hampton, "this summer taught me a lesson I hope I'll never forget."

By 1898 Susan was the busy mother of two little boys, Caryl and Pierre, and she had returned to her work as doctor, teacher, nurse, financial and legal adviser, translator, and fighter in the battle against alcohol. Somehow Susan did it all.

In her spare moments, Susan would pile the boys, her mother (gently), and her sewing into the buggy or the old wagon and drive over to Rosalie's crowded, noisy, comfortable house filled with seven children. On her way back from a patient, Susan might stop her buggy at Rosalie's to help with her sister's never-ending cooking, sewing, washing, and cleaning. And when one of Rosalie's children fell out of the hayloft and broke a leg or stepped on a nail or got burned with the boiling wash water, Susan would be there as fast as her horse could go.

Susan on the porch of her home in Bancroft with her mother and two sons, Caryl and Pierre

Wherever her buggy or her wagon was, there came Omahas in need. Perhaps, seeing Susan's buggy, Prairie Chicken would drop by for advice. Perhaps Little Chief would stop in so Susan could translate a paper into Omaha for him. Perhaps Mrs. Fire Chief needed a new bottle of medicine. Whatever the need, Susan would put her work aside with a smile, step over a child or two, and get the job done.

The next five years were happy ones for Susan. All the loves she had when she was little, she had still— her family, her pony, the prairie, and making life better for her people. Sometimes the problems seemed un-ending, especially the alcohol problem, but Susan tried not to feel disheartened. She tackled the tribe's troubles with a mixture of cheerful good humor, outraged anger, and sometimes grim determination.

There was one problem Susan had, however, that even her utmost determination could not seem to solve. This problem became a growing, glowering black shadow on her family's happiness, in her own home. And it was alcohol.

In 1905 Susan's husband, Henry, died of alcoholism, the same disease she had been speaking against so hard and for so long. Susan was brokenhearted and lonely and very, very discouraged. Her friends gave her a "world full of love and sympathy," she wrote, "but there are times when I get so lonely and want to see him so much." She wished desperately that she "could only turn time back a little," but that was impossible, even for the dauntless Susan. So she and her two little boys, ages seven and nine, moved from the house with its sweet-smelling flowers and big garden to a house in Macy at the Omaha Agency, and they started over.

VII
One More Battle

It wasn't long before Susan was busier than ever. In addition to her usual duties, she was now caring for her elderly, sick mother, and in 1905 she was appointed as a Presbyterian missionary to the Omaha tribe. So Susan LaFlesche Picotte, who was the first Indian woman doctor, was also the first Indian—man or woman—ever chosen to be a missionary. It had been many years since the embarrassing church wedding, and now Susan had a little more success in persuading the Omahas to try the Christian religion. The first Sunday she spoke, three people were in church. The next Sunday there were twenty-five, and more came every Sunday to hear Susan read the Bible in Omaha and translate the hymns. In her care, the Sunday school and church grew and blossomed and thrived.

In 1906 Susan bought land on the reservation in the new town of Walthill, very close to land that Marguerite and her husband bought. The workmen who built Susan's tall new house were amazed at all the windows she wanted, but she explained that plenty of air and sunshine was the best medicine.

Susan had frequent family dinners and parties and luncheons for friends and neighbors, both Indian and white. She would tie a big white apron over her dress and cook in her sunny new kitchen. She planted flowers and fruit trees around her new house, and she shared whatever she had. Her Indian patients usually paid with vegetables, which was helpful, because Susan didn't have much time to garden.

Susan was always finding new ways to help her people. She helped organize the county medical society, was a member of the state medical society, and served as chairwoman of the state health committee. She spoke again and again about the need for a hospital on the reservation, but there still wasn't enough money, so she kept the idea in the back of her mind and turned to other concerns. She went to the state capital at Lincoln to speak to lawmakers about stronger health laws. She also went by train from Walthill to Washington, D.C., and spoke before the secretary of the interior. As a result, a law was passed to ensure that no alcohol could be sold, ever, in the new towns of Walthill and Rosalie, on the reservation. Unfortunately "ever" lasted for only fifty years before the law was voted down.

Susan was now called by others the Omahas' bridge from the old to the new, just as she had dreamed.

Susan's home in Walthill (left) was always open and often overflowing with grown-ups and children. Over the fireplace (below), Susan put the saying, "East, West, Hame's [Home's] Best."

People said she was the Omahas' "best and truest friend." Her name came to mean right and justice, and the *Southern Workman* newspaper reported that she stood "as a strong wall" between the Omahas and those who would harm them.

There was no denying the importance of Susan LaFlesche Picotte to the Omahas. She led and advised them, just as her father had done. Years later the *New York Sun* newspaper wrote that Susan was "virtual chief without having the title. Her word was higher law in the tribe than that of the Indian agent."

Susan's aged mother, Mary, died in 1909 after many years of poor health. Susan was often quite sick, too, with those same painful earaches and backaches that had started during her first winter's rides to see patients. Even though she was a doctor, Susan could not cure the pains in her own head. She often had trouble eating, and sometimes she needed a nurse herself. But even when she had to stay in bed, her pen was busy. Actually, she wrote so many letters that she exchanged her pen for a typewriter and pounded away from morning to night. Susan wrote to lawmakers and congressmen about the continuing concerns of the Omaha people, who were trying to make progress despite government paperwork that would choke a buffalo.

"We have rules and regulations to the right of us, to the left of us, behind us," she typed in December 1909, "do you wonder we object to . . . them in front of us?" The Indian agent, or Susan herself, had to write to Washington with each separate request from each person for the use of his or her own money, whether that person wanted to buy a blanket or a wagon. Even food shopping was not a simple matter. "If the department approves the number and size of prunes bought," Susan typed sarcastically, "and the color of the bananas, the government pays the bill out of the Indian's own money."

She would gladly help the United States government in any way for the welfare of her tribe, Susan wrote, but she would "always fight good and hard" if it was against her tribe. Susan's typewriter keys slammed onto the paper. She would fight, she said, even "if I have to fight alone, for before my God I owe my people a responsibility."

She spoke to small groups and large groups, from Sunday school classes on the Omaha Reservation to congressional committees in Washington, D.C. Those who heard her said she could make the oldest, most intricate stories come to life, and when she wanted to win an argument, she was clear and logical and forceful. And she usually won.

In 1910 Susan won a remarkably large victory. Her letters and newspaper articles had not been enough to sway the government from its belief that Indians were children who couldn't manage their own affairs. So in February, Susan went to Washington, D.C. She hadn't really wanted to go to Washington at all, but when she refused, some of the Omahas threatened to carry her to the train and put her on. In Washington she argued before the attorney general and the secretary of the

Susan in her late forties

interior that the Omahas were just as competent as white people and should certainly be able to take care of their own money. And so it came to be. The *Fremont Tribune* wrote in March 1910, "Dr. Picotte . . . drew up a second declaration of independence" in winning the right for the Omahas to control their own property.

There were smaller victories, too. There was the battle against the Common Drinking Cup. At that time, people shared the same drinking cup when they got a drink of water, which meant that they were also sharing their germs. Susan wrote articles explaining why this was not healthy, and soon people began to use disposable paper cups instead. Then there was the battle against the Fly. Susan's energetic lessons about keeping clean and using screens to cover food had some effect, for although flies were not eradicated, at least they didn't find as many landing places.

Susan was invited back to Hampton in the spring of 1910 but couldn't go because she was feeling awful ("on the edge of the precipice," she described it). But still she pushed herself to do what she could for the Omahas.

In September 1910, Susan wrote in her diary that, besides her doctoring and nursing work, she interpreted, explained legal papers, settled arguments, wrote letters, collected rents, and kept financial records for Yellow Fox, Little Cook, White Horse, Big Black Bear, Little Turkey, Mrs. Fire Chief, Good Old Man, Little Soldier, and Rabbit. She wrote articles for local newspapers about tribal customs, Indian farming, and legends about corn. She played hymns and preached sermons and named babies and cooked meals for her patients. She took raspberries, peaches, asparagus, and peas to people in need. One day, sadly, she took a little white dress with ribbons to a grieving mother, whose dead baby was then buried in the white dress. And this was just a typical month for Susan.

It was good that Susan was so busy, because she was very lonesome. That same month, her two sons left home to enter the Nebraska Military Academy, in Lincoln. She thought they would receive the best education there, but she missed them terribly. She took the train to Lincoln to see them as often as she could.

Sometimes Susan got to ride in an automobile, but she really preferred a good horse. Summer and winter, when she wasn't on horseback, Susan drove her horse and buggy. One fine autumn day, she drove fifty miles. Another morning she went out at dawn to ride alone. When she returned, breathless with joy, she said it was the most beautiful morning she had ever seen on the prairie. The air was soft and sweet, the dirt road long and smooth, and her heart was content.

But there was one more battle to win.

Ever since she had been a student at Hampton, Susan had hoped and expected that her people would some day have a hospital of their own. She had tried again and again to raise enough money herself, but was disappointed again and again. So Susan treated her patients as best she could without a hospital, and she sent only the worst cases to Omaha, Nebraska, or Sioux City, Iowa, for operations or difficult medical treatments. Often it was the oldest people who needed to go to a hospital in "a civilization new to them," as Susan said, but they felt lost and frightened when they were away from home, and many never recovered.

Now, with new towns and railroads spreading over the reservation, Susan tried again. With the support of a new white doctor, Susan and the whole community, Indian and white, finally raised ten thousand dollars for the hospital and all its equipment.

The hospital was built on a hilltop in Walthill, with

The Dr. Susan Picotte Memorial Hospital, Walthill, Nebraska, was placed on the National Register of Historic Places in 1989.

lots of windows, just as Susan wanted. One whole side of the top floor was an open porch with hammocks and beds, where the patients could recover in the fresh air and sunshine ("nature's medicine," Susan called it). Susan was the doctor in charge of the whole hospital, which was to serve both Indians and whites, side by side. The hospital opened in January 1913.

In the spring of 1915, Susan had to have two operations on the bones of her face, which had ached so painfully for many years. The operations were not successful.

Susan died in September 1915, in her own home, with her family around her. She was only fifty years old. As she had asked, the closing prayer for her funeral service was given in the Omaha language, by an aged Omaha man.

The local newspapers had to print additional pages to report all the kind words Susan's friends and co-workers had to say about her.

But just before she died, Susan said quietly, "I cannot see how any credit is due me. I am thankful I've been called and permitted to serve. I feel blessed for that privilege above all measure."

Afterword

Today the Omaha Indians are intent upon relearning their rich heritage as they move toward a cultural renaissance.

Although from Iron Eye's time forward, many Omahas attempted to make a transition to the white culture, most ended up stuck somewhere in between—without either old *or* new. Fortunately, in spite of upheaval and change and loss, the Omahas quietly retained belief in their heritage. The recent return of the Sacred Pole, the creation of the Susan LaFlesche Picotte Center, and the work of the Omaha Historical Research Project have helped create a renewal of traditional values within the Omaha tribe.

Notes

page 6

Susan LaFlesche Picotte's name is pronounced lah-FLESH pee-COT.

page 8

The word *Indian* has been used to tell Susan LaFlesche Picotte's story because that is the word she used to describe herself. Many people now prefer the term *Native American.*

page 10

The U.S. Department of the Interior managed Indian affairs by appointing agents to handle trade and other transactions on Indian reservations.

page 14

Iron Eye's role as chief continues to cause great controversy within the Omaha tribe. Some feel he did a great disservice to the Omahas by stressing the need to adopt white ways, rather than encouraging traditional ways and values.

page 23

Many people now believe that the destruction of Indian culture was the ultimate goal of the white man's education.

page 30

Susan's oldest sister, Susette, spent her entire adult life speaking before white audiences to persuade them that Indians were people with rights and feelings. At one point she wrote bitterly, "I often wonder if there is anything in your civilization which will make good to us what we have lost."

page 48

The aged Omaha men were finally convinced that the buffalo would never return. They discussed what to do with the sacred objects for each ceremony, such as the Sacred Pole, the Sacred Tent of War, and the Sacred White Buffalo Hide. They decided that the last man in charge of each object would care for it until his death, when it would be buried with him and the old ways would pass out of existence.

Francis LaFlesche and Alice Fletcher were able to obtain the Sacred Pole and the Sacred Tent of War for the Peabody Museum at Yale University. This created great ill feeling within the tribe, and coincidentally Iron Eye died suddenly a few months after the Sacred Pole was removed. The Sacred Pole was returned to the Omahas in 1989.

page 61

Rich white speculators bought up valuable Omaha land, sometimes honestly, usually not. This removed not only the hope but even the possibility of Omahas becoming productive, successful farmers. Saddest of all, too often an Indian sold land for quick cash to spend on alcohol or to pay bills that had been run up at the trader's store.

page 79

An unstrung bow is a traditional Indian symbol for death. This is an especially appropriate symbol to use to mark the end of Susan LaFlesche Picotte's life, because the name LaFlesche means "the arrow" in French.

Bibliography

Books:

Barnes, R. H. *Two Crows Denies It: A History of Controversy in Omaha Sociology*. Lincoln, Nebraska: University of Nebraska Press, 1984.

Brown, Marion Marsh. *Homeward the Arrow's Flight*. Nashville, Tennessee: Abingdon, 1980.

Crary, Margaret. *Susette LaFlesche: Voice of the Omaha Indians*. New York: Hawthorne Books, 1973.

Fichter, George S. *How the Plains Indians Lived*. New York: David McKay Co., 1980.

Freedman, Russell. *Buffalo Hunt*. New York: Holiday House, 1988.

Green, Norma Kidd. *Iron Eye's Family: The Children of Joseph LaFlesche*. Lincoln, Nebraska: Johnsen Publishing Co., 1969.

Gridley, Marion E. *American Indian Women*. New York: Hawthorne Books, 1974.

Hyde, George E. *The Pawnee Indians*. Norman, Oklahoma: University of Oklahoma Press, 1951.

LaFlesche, Francis. *The Middle Five: Indian Schoolboys*. 1900. Reprint. Lincoln, Nebraska: University of Nebraska Press, 1963.

LaFlesche, Francis, and Alice Fletcher. *The Omaha Tribe*. 2 vols. 1911. Reprint. Lincoln, Nebraska: University of Nebraska Press, 1972.

Milner, Clyde A., II. *With Good Intentions: Quaker Work Among the Pawnees, Otos, and Omahas in the 1870s*. Lincoln, Nebraska: University of Nebraska Press, 1982.

Simmons, Jerold, ed. *"La Belle Vue": Studies in the History of Bellevue, Nebraska*. Missouri: Walsworth Publishing, 1976.

Smith, G. Hubert. *Omaha Indians (Indian Claims Commissions Findings)*. New York: Garland Publishing, 1974.

Articles:

Mathes, Valerie Sherer. "Susan LaFlesche Picotte: Nebraska's Indian Physician, 1865-1915." *Nebraska History* 63 (1982).

Nebraska State Historical Society. "40 Years Among the Indians on the Eastern Borders of Nebraska." Transactions of the Nebraska State Historical Society, 1887.

Street, Douglas. "LaFlesche Sisters Write to *St. Nicolas Magazine*." *Nebraska History* 62 (1981).

Manuscripts:

LaFlesche Family Papers. Nebraska State Historical Society, Lincoln, Nebraska.

Letters Received from Susan LaFlesche, 1886-1893. Record Group 75. Bureau of Indian Affairs. National Archives and Records Service, Washington, D.C.

Papers of Susan LaFlesche Picotte. Nebraska State Historical Society, Lincoln, Nebraska.

Susan LaFlesche Letters. Hampton Institute Archives, Hampton, Virginia.

Susan LaFlesche Picotte Alumna File and Women's Medical College Faculty Minutes. The Medical College of Pennsylvania, Philadelphia.

Interviews with Author:

Edwards, Rae. Granddaughter of Marguerite LaFlesche. Walthill, Nebraska, June 1989.

Farley, Dr. Rosalie. Granddaughter of Rosalie LaFlesche. Lincoln, Nebraska, June 1989.

Hastings, Dennis. Omaha Historian, Omaha Tribe of Nebraska. Macy, Nebraska, June 1989.

Langenberg, Margory. Daughter of Marguerite LaFlesche. Walthill, Nebraska, June 1989.

All quotations in this biography were taken from the above sources.

Index

My special thanks to Mr. Dennis Hastings, Historian, Omaha Tribe, for his ongoing generous assistance in assuring the accuracy of my research; to Dr. Troy R. Johnson, Book Review Editor, *American Indian Culture and Research Journal*, University of California, Los Angeles, for his helpful and specific comments related to Indian cultural matters; and to Dr. Rosalie Farley and Mrs. Rae Edwards, grandnieces of Susan LaFlesche Picotte, for their graciously given interviews and joyously guided tours.

The illustrations are reproduced through the courtesy of: pp. 2, 6, 14 (left and right), 29, 37, 55, 68, 72 (top and bottom), 75, 78, Nebraska State Historical Society; p. 9, Chicago and North Western Railway; pp. 17, 57, 66, Smithsonian Institution National Anthropological Archives; pp. 22, Independent Picture Source; p. 25, Glenbow Photographs; pp. 34, 38 (top and bottom), Hampton University Archival and Museum Collection, Hampton University, Hampton, Virginia; p. 41, The Historical Society of Pennsylvania; p. 45 (top and bottom), Archives and Special Collections on Women in Medicine, Medical College of Pennsylvania, Philadelphia, Pennsylvania; p. 62, Library of Congress. Cover photographs courtesy of Nebraska State Historical Society (inset) and Independent Picture Source.